NATURE ADAPTED

Guidebook for evaluating and modifying programs and practices to increase outdoor accessibility

Created by:

Patti Bonnin

First paperback edition July 2024
ISBN 9798332430084
Independently published

Graphics designed through Canva

Dedication:

For our son.
We are breaking down
barriers for you.

CONTENTS

Acknowledgements

Originally, *Nature Adapted* was written for my Masters Degree as part of a Capstone graduation requirement. My amazing professor Trish Harvey and my EE group mates, Nicole Bolduc and Evangeline Holley, all provided invaluable feedback and support during the research and writing phase. Jessica Burke from Texas Parks and Wildlife Department served as content reviewer for my paper as well as this guidebook, and her enthusiasm and encouragement convinced me to redesigned this into an actual book. Also, a special thanks to the Houston Arboretum & Nature Center and Jesse H. Jones Park for letting me pick your brains on accessibility in the outdoors.

Most of all I want to give the biggest THANK YOU to my husband, mom, sister, and the rest of my family who have listened to me ramble on non-stop about this book to the point where you were glossy-eyed and tired. You have been my biggest fans and strongest supporters, and I could not have done this without you!

FOREWORD

This guidebook is intended to help nature centers and organizations who specialize in outdoor education and recreation to better understand how people with disabilities interact with the natural world. Every person deserves the opportunity to explore and enjoy nature, but outdoor spaces tend to have more barriers than access for people with disabilities. By reading through this guidebook, I hope you are inspired and motivated to find ways to increase the accessibility of your organization's practices to be more inclusive for the disability community.

Along with an introduction of disability and accessibility terms, the book is divided into the different sections of physical site review, educational programming, website transparency, and workplace inclusivity. Each section begins with a pre-assessment for you to complete. This allows you to consider what accessibility tools and resources you currently offer and gives you ideas of what you could potentially offer in the future. The sections end with an opportunity to reflect on the key takeaways from the information and provides you with a place to jot down ideas for improving your organization's programming or practices, as well as think about any potential barriers or challenges you may encounter along the way.

Section 1: Defining Disabilities and Accessibility

Pre-Assessment

What does it mean to be disabled?

What is accessibility ?

What is the ADA?

Why is accessibility in the outdoors important?

What are barriers to access?

Can you think of any barriers to access your organization has?

What is the difference between accessibility and usability?

Do the ADA laws apply to outdoor spaces?

Defining Disabilities and Accessibility

Disability

The term disability is often used to describe a person with a physical disability. In actuality, disability refers to a group of people with a wide range of varying medical conditions and special needs. A disability is an impairment that limits a major life activity for that person, such as difficulties with walking, breathing, lifting, communicating, concentrating or thinking and processing. Examples of physical disabilities include missing or partial limbs, vision impairment, hearing loss, spinal cord injuries, cerebral palsy, traumatic brain injuries, communication disorders, and epilepsy. Disabilities also include neurodevelopmental disorders like Autism spectrum disorder, attention-deficit hyperactivity disorder, intellectual disorders, and mental health disorders such as anxiety and sensory processing disorders. Do not judge a disability by its visibility. Not all disabilities or disorders can be physically seen.

It is worth noting that disabilities, illnesses, and disorders will present differently for each person. Someone's disability is unique to their own health conditions, personal experiences, environmental factors, lifestyle restrictions, and limitations to activities. Thus, the accommodations and level of accessibility required will vary depending on the specific needs of the individual at any given time.

Accessibility

The goal of accessibility is to provide participants with the tools, resources, and environments necessary to engage equally and effectively in programs. Accessibility concepts are dynamic and complicated in practice. As mentioned above, disabilities can present in a myriad of ways therefore requiring each person to have specialized tools and resources to assist them. There is no one-size-fits-all approach to meeting the needs of the disability community. This obviously makes it more difficult when modifying programs to be more inclusive, but the effort is important.

Importance of Accessible Outdoor Programs

People with disabilities benefit greatly from time spent outdoors. Active lifestyles in natural settings have been shown to provide numerous physical and mental health benefits, and have a positive effect on one's intellectual, emotional, social, and spiritual well-being. These health gains are even more important for people with medical conditions. Increased time in nature can help people feel more balanced, have increased feelings of meaningfulness and vitality, boost the immune system, and increase one's self-esteem and confidence.

Barriers

Despite the importance of having access to nature, the reality is that most people with disabilities are faced with challenges when exploring the outdoors. These may include physical barriers, attitudinal barriers, social barriers, communication barriers, policy barriers, and a lack of consistent resources for people with physical disabilities, making it more difficult to find the motivation to venture outdoors. Throughout the next few sections, we will look at some of the common barriers and challenges people with disabilities encounter while spending time outdoors or attending environmental education programming.

Usability

The Americans with Disabilities Act (ADA) established in 1990 was designed to protect the civil rights for people with disabilities. Businesses and organizations open to the public are required to adhere to these laws in order to provide equal access and opportunities for everyone. Examples include having accessible parking spots, doorways wide enough for wheelchair access, accessible bathrooms, or providing reasonable accommodations in the workplace. The problem is there is a difference between the accessibility requirements by the ADA and the level of usability by the people. While businesses are required to have 1 accessible parking spot for every 25 spots, having additional parking or van accessible parking is more user-friendly. You may have a doorway that is of the correct width for wheelchairs but have doors so heavy that people with upper body mobility issues struggle to open them or have a high threshold that is a trip hazard for people using mobility aids. Thus, it is important to consider how people will actually use your facilities, trails, and participate in your programs. Should you follow ADA laws and requirements? Absolutely! But consider these laws to be more of a bare-minimum approach and strive to find a way to be more functionable for your patrons.

As you complete the upcoming Reflections portions at the end of each section, think about the ADA laws. Are you or someone in your organization familiar with the legal requirements under the Americans with Disabilities Act? For instance, can you legally deny access to a service animal? Can you tell someone who is deaf or hard of hearing that you don't offer interpretive services? Do requirements for accessible pathways apply to trail systems? Do you know where you can find resources for organizations regarding disabilities and accessibilities? (Hint! Check out the back of this guidebook for help getting started!)

Reflections

What are some of the key takeaways from this section?

Looking at your pre-assessment, is there something your organization currently does not offer that you think it could? Or is there something you do offer that can be improved?

Are there any barriers you need to overcome to put these practices into use? These barriers may include lack of funding, need for additional staffing, increased training for staff and volunteers, or simply not knowing where to start.

Section 2: Physical Site Review

Pre-Assessment

TRAILS:

Number of total trails?

Number of accessible trails?

Ground surfaces of accessible trails?

Ground surfaces of non-accessible trails?

Are the trails loops, out-and-back, or lollipop?

Are the trails regularly maintained?

Is there trail signage?

    Is accessible information listed on there (distance, surfaces, slopes)?

Are there trail maps located on the trail?

    Are they offered in digital form?

    Are they tactile?

    Are they offered in braille, large print, or have an audio option?

    Are trails color-coded, labelled, or both?

    Are benches, rest areas, and accessible facilities clearly designated on map?

How much of the trail is shaded?

Do trails have pullouts for rest stops?

Are there benches for resting?

    With armrests?

    With backrests?

    Are they connected to the trail with an accessible surface?

    How often will benches be encountered?

Are there trail obstacles (large rocks, roots, ruts, etc)?

Are there any slopes? What grade are they?

Are there gates or bollards blocking paths?

Are there picnic tables?

      Do they have extended tables and spaces for wheelchair access?

      Is the ground surface up to and surrounding the table accessible?

Is there a play area?

      What are the ground surfaces?

      Are there accessible play features?

      Are there sensory features?

Are there fishing piers?

      Do the railings allow for a clear line of sight at wheelchair height?

      Are they wheelchair accessible?

Are the trails popular or have very few visitors?

What are the peak times of day/week/year?

Who else uses the trails (horses, cyclists, mountain bikes, dirt bikes, golf carts, etc)?

Are there large parties or gatherings allowed?

Is the area noisy with traffic, construction, airports, factories, farms, firing ranges, hunting, or play areas?

Additional safety concerns:

      Are dogs or other animals allowed?

      Are there insects like mosquitoes, ticks, chiggers?

      Are there large animals like mountain lions, bears, or wolves?

      Is the general area high in crime?

BUILDINGS:

What buildings are open to the public?

Is there a visitor center?

Are there staff, volunteers, or rangers on-site for questions or an emergency?

Are there accessible doors and entryways to the buildings?

Are there automatic doors?

Are the doors heavy and/or hard to open?

Is there a threshold to transverse?

Are there bathrooms?

Are there wheelchair accessible bathrooms?

Are the accessible bathrooms only open when the building is open?

Are the sinks, hand soaps, dryers, and mirrors at wheelchair accessible heights?

Are there adult changing tables?

Is there a café or a place for people to purchase food or drinks?

Are there water fountains?

Are they accessible?

Are they inside or outside?

Are they available after building closing hours?

What other structures do you have?

Are they accessible?

PARKING:

What is the surface type of the parking lot?

Are there potholes or muddy areas?

How many total number of parking spaces are there?

How many are accessible parking spots?

How many are van accessible?

Is the accessible parking on a flat surface or a slope?

Is the parking lot well-lit at night?

Are there curb cuts on the sidewalks?

Are the sidewalks at least 36 inches? Or 60 inches?

Are there stairs in or around the building or grounds?

How many steps?

Are the steps slippery when wet?

Are there ramps in or around the building or grounds?

Physical Site Review

As you begin to take a closer look at your physical site, it is important to clarify what is legally required and what is not. The American Disabilities Act (ADA) specifically refers to areas open to the public, like parking lots, buildings, restrooms, and access paths to buildings. However, trail systems and outdoor areas are not included in these requirements. There are guidelines for accessibility in park systems, but they are only a requirement for federal lands and park systems and are merely offered as optional guidelines for local, state, or private outdoor areas. Written by the U.S. Forest Service and the U.S. Department of Agriculture, the *Accessibility Guidebook for Outdoor Recreation and Trails* (2012) provides a wealth of information regarding accessibility in the outdoors and is a highly recommended resource.

Parking

Let's start with the one of the first points of access for visitors: parking lots. The ADA requires 1 accessible parking spot for every 25 spots on site. There are also requirements for widths, ground markings, access aisles, slopes, and surfaces. The best way to ensure that you are meeting the minimum requirements for accessibility under the Americans with Disabilities Act is to visit their website. However, doing more than the bare minimum is strongly encouraged. Having only 1 accessible parking spot limits groups of people who want to attend outings together. Other issues to consider for parking lots are the ground surfaces and the slope. Parking lots with a dirt or grass surface are vulnerable to potholes, ruts, or become muddy when wet. It is also important that there are aisles next to the accessible parking spots. This allows people with mobility aids like wheelchairs, scooters, and walkers to have a safe place to unload and maneuver around their vehicles. Sidewalks in the parking lots, as well as throughout the property, should be at least 36 inches for one-way traffic, 60 inches for two-way traffic, and have curb cuts for easy access. Curb cuts not only benefit mobility aid users, but also people with vision impairment, strollers, kids on bicycles, and people pushing carts or wagons. It is also important that your parking lots and sidewalks are well-lit at night to help people navigate around easier.

Facilities

All facilities, not just the buildings open to the public, should be accessible. This includes having ramps available when there are steps, elevators if there is more than one floor, appropriate lighting, accessible bathrooms and water fountains, and preferably automatic doors. Doors that are heavy may be difficult to open for people who use mobility aids or who may have weak upper body strength from conditions like cerebral palsy. Having pronounced thresholds in the doorways can also create obstacles for people with lower body mobility issues.

Trail Surfaces

Not all ground surfaces are accessible to everyone. Trail surfaces that are considered accessible are pavement, asphalt, boardwalks, and packed, crushed granite. Surfaces that are not considered accessible include mulch, grass, loose gravel, rocks, sand, and dirt or soil. Keep in mind that accessibility is different for everyone and therefore, not all trails will be accessible for all people. For example, a person with sensory issues, who tire easy, or with weak muscle tone may not wish to transverse the bumpy boardwalks or granite. Instead, they may prefer a smoother surface of paved trails.

Rest Stops

A pullout is an area along the side of the trail that offers a place for people using mobility devices to pull off on the side of the trail to rest, take in the view, or to allow other visitors to pass by. They are especially helpful for trails that are less than 60 inches wide. Knowing the location of benches along the route is also helpful for people with chronic fatigue syndrome or may be recovering from surgery. Benches with backrests and armrests give the guests support when sitting. It is also important that the benches are located on an accessible trail surface to ensure access to them.

Trail Obstacles

Obstacles like tree roots, ruts, broken asphalt, large rocks, gates, or bollards can hinder a person's access to the trails. These obstacles should be removed or clearly stated on the maps and trail signage to warn people ahead of time.

Trail Maps

Maps should be offered in various forms to be inclusive for people who are visually impaired. This could include having versions that are tactile, have audio options, larger print, or in a digital form for them to enlarge on their phones or tablets. Trails should also be identified by labels or symbols, not just color-coded, for people with color blindness. On the map, accessible features like locations of benches, bathrooms, and water fountains, should be identified.

Trail Signage

Trail signage can be especially important if trail maps are not readily available or if they do not contain all of the pertinent accessibility information for that trail. Trail signage may include information such as ground surfaces, potential obstacles, length of trail, slope of trail, and any stairs or ramps along the trail. The more information you can provide ahead of time can make a significant difference to people with disabilities. It can be frustrating for people to get part of the way down a trail only to find out the slope is too steep or there is large rock in the path that is impassable for them.

Additional Safety Concerns

Safety on trails is a concern for many people, not just those with disabilities. While this is not an exhaustive list by any means, it is a place to start. Here are some common safety issues to consider:

- Is there someone available in case of an emergency (staff, rangers, volunteers, etc)?
- Are there large crowds that people may wish to avoid? Or do your trails have low visitorship which may be concerning for people who do not wish to be outdoors alone?
- Are there insects like mosquitoes, ticks, or chiggers?
- What animals might they encounter that could be dangerous? What suggestions do you have for visitors who encounter these animals?
- Are dogs allowed? Keep in mind that many people are afraid of dogs and some religions forbid the touching of dogs.
- Some visitors may be sensitive to loud noises. For example, hearing gun fire from a nearby firing range may be a trigger for people with Post-traumatic stress disorder. While some people prefer quieter areas, others may find the silence uncomfortable.

Reflections

What are some of the key takeaways from this section?

Looking at your pre-assessment, is there something your organization currently does not offer that you think it could? Or is there something you do offer that can be improved?

Are there any barriers you need to overcome to put these practices into use? These barriers may include lack of funding, need for additional staffing, increased training for staff and volunteers, or simply not knowing where to start.

Section 3: Inclusive Educational Programming

Pre-Assessment

Do you offer educational programming?

What age range are the programs geared towards?

Do you have strict age limits on programming?

Where are the programs held? Are there indoor options available?

Do you offer alternative activities for people with disabilities?

Do you offer programs designed specifically for people with disabilities or special needs?

Is registration required for programming?

Can people request accommodations? If so, how?

Are caregivers or aides allowed to attend programs to assist participants?

Do you offer adaptive gear for outdoor activities? If so, what?

Do you have tables or sensory bins that are wheelchair accessible?

Are larger activities broken down into small steps to make them easier to understand?

Are instructions and safety concerns repeated throughout the lesson?

Are ideas and concepts taught in a variety of ways to accommodate different learning styles?

Are activities planned based on chronological age, developmental age, or both?

Is sensory exploration encouraged throughout the program?

Do you offer materials that are tactile or brightly colored?

Are visual cues or tactile boundaries placed for people with visual impairments?

Do you offer interpreter or other services for people who are hearing impaired?

Are there built-in rest periods for those who fatigue easy or need additional time to complete tasks?

Is curriculum differentiated to adapt to varying levels of ability?

Are there a variety of sensory options for people who prefer to touch or not to touch specific textures?

Are there options for participants who are nonverbal or with communication disorders to be able to participate?

Do you engage with the disability community, organizations, or consultants for feedback and input on programming and policies?

Is program success based on outcomes or the process?

Inclusive Educational Programming

Getting people outdoors is one of the biggest goals for nature centers and outdoor recreation organizations. However, many programs offered by outdoor places are not disability-friendly, mainly because most outdoor spaces were not originally designed with disabilities in mind. Creating a truly inclusive program can be daunting due to the vast variety of types of disabilities that people experience. It is important to keep in mind it is nearly impossible to design an outdoor program that is 100% accessible for every person. And that is okay! The goal is to try to be as inclusive as possible, modify what you can, be open to new ideas, and be honest about your limitations when people ask for accommodations. If you are teaching a hunting class, it is going to be loud. Ear protection may reduce, but may not completely eliminate, the loud noises of the guns firing. If someone has a sensory issues related to noise levels, this may not be an activity they can participate in.

Create a Checklist

When developing programming, making a checklist of elements you want to focus on and adding possible ways to accommodate accessibility requests can be helpful. For example, is your program sensory-friendly? Can your program have an indoor option or be in a shaded area if needed for people who are sensitive to the sun? Do you have a way to communicate your information to people who are deaf, have vision impairments, or who have communication disorders if needed? Are the instructions for your activities delivered in small steps to make it easier for people with intellectual disabilities to follow along? Are you able to present the information or instructions in different ways to help people with learning disabilities or processing disorders to better understand them? Keeping some of these questions in mind will help when developing an inclusive program.

Sensory Elements

Environmental education tends to be sensory-based and naturally immersive. Splashing in puddles, touching fuzzy leaves, playing in sand, listening for birds, planting in soil, feeling the sunshine and wind, and seeing colorful flowers and butterflies are all wonderful sensory experiences. When deciding what sensory elements to include in your programming, remember that everyone has a different reaction to sensory items. For example, one child may love the feel of squishy mud and another child be repulsed by it. Some people may be overwhelmed experiencing the new sights and unfamiliar sounds of the natural world. While most people do find nature calming and restorative, there are some who may struggle being outside of their normal routine and familiar settings. It is great to encourage people to try new things but keep in mind that they may have their own level of comfort with certain activities.

Possible Accommodations

For children with disabilities who attend schools, they may be receiving accommodations from their district to help them maneuver around the campus and to facilitate their learning. When attending camps or outdoor programming, they may find the lack of accommodations difficult. As an organization who has educational programs, this is something you may want to learn more about. What types of accommodations do you already offer? What are some additional accommodations you could provide? Some common ones may include needing a buddy or aide to help them complete activities, repeating instructions often, breaking instructions down into smaller steps, allowing additional breaks to rest, having shorter hikes, using accessible trails, providing a snack time (especially important for people with diabetes), having a calm corner or sensory kits for people who are overwhelmed, and having adaptive gear available for activities such as kayaking, fishing, or hunting. Also, having flexibility on age limits is important for children with intellectual disabilities. A child's chronological age may be 8 years old, but their intellectual or developmental age may be more in line with that of a 3 year old. If there are strict age requirements for your programs, it is helpful for parents to know that in advance so they can make the decision if this will be a good fit for their child.

Financial Barriers

One barrier to spending time in outdoor recreation is the cost of purchasing and storing adaptive gear. If you need adaptive paddles for kayaking, a tripod to hold your binoculars when birding, or specialty fishing rods, it can be expensive to purchase the necessary items. This is why having them available for your participants can be one less barrier for them to overcome. If you don't have a high demand for adaptive gear, consider reaching out to other nearby outdoor recreational centers to see if they have items you can borrow. Additionally, check around your city for a local lending library that may have adaptive gear available for checkout. You may also want to consider offering a discount for programs or memberships for people with disabilities. For example, the National Park Service has an Access Pass that allows people with permanent disabilities free lifetime access to their parks. This may not be possible for smaller organizations or non-profits who depend on the income supplied by programming, memberships, or parking fees. One suggestion to offset costs of programming is to team up with local organizations who might be willing to help cover the costs of supplies or provide volunteers to help programs that are geared towards increasing outdoor accessibility.

Additional Thoughts

So, you may be asking yourself, how in the world are you supposed to be able to accommodate every possible disability? And the answer is you probably couldn't, and you don't have to! Not every program is a good fit for every person, and not every activity can be easily adapted. One way to help prepare yourself and the participants is to have information for the class available in advance and to allow people the opportunity to ask for accommodations before or during registration. This will give you the chance to evaluate your program to make adjustments, or let the participants know if this is something you can not accommodate. Please keep in mind that some accommodations, like providing assistance to people who are vision impaired, allowing service animals to attend, or have interpreters for those who are deaf/hard of hearing, may be legally required. Other accommodations, like longer program times or providing all-terrain wheelchairs, are optional. It is strongly recommended that you familiarize yourself with the local, state, and federal laws regarding disabilities, services, and accommodations for your area.

Reflections

What are some of the key takeaways from this section?

Looking at your pre-assessment, is there something your organization currently does not offer that you think it could? Or is there something you do offer that can be improved?

Are there any barriers you need to overcome to put these practices into use? These barriers may include lack of funding, need for additional staffing, increased training for staff and volunteers, or simply not knowing where to start.

Section 4: Creating an Accessible Workplace

Pre-Assessment

What are the backgrounds of the staff?

Are any trained in ADA, disability services, or special education training?

Do you have an Accessibility Coordinator, or similar position?

Does your organization have an Equal Opportunity Policy, or similar policy?

Does leadership work to maintain a culture of inclusion?

Do you have a physically safe working environment for people with disabilities?

Does your organization offer accommodations for staff if needed?

Can staff or volunteers modify their work environment as needed?

Is there a clearly stated policy instructing people how to request accommodations?

Do you offer IDEA (Inclusion, Diversity, Equality, Accessibility) trainings for staff and/or

volunteers?

Do you offer volunteer accommodations?

Examples:

Do you track requests for accommodations for staff, volunteers, guests, or program

participants? If so, how?

Do you hire staff with special needs?

Do you permit people with disabilities to volunteer?

Do you have any rules or limitations for volunteers with disabilities?

Do you have adaptive gear or tools available for staff or volunteers to use?

Are flexible work arrangements for staff and/or volunteers an option?

Have you applied for and/or received grants related to accessibility or inclusion?

Does your organization have any specific goals related to IDEA?

Do you have a board of directors?

      What are their views on IDEA?

Creating an Accessible Workplace

Building an organization that is truly inclusive to everyone also means providing accommodations for your staff and volunteers. This includes everyone from the administration team and board of directors to your employees, part-time contractors, and volunteers. By establishing a culture of inclusion, you are demonstrating positive attitudes and acceptance towards people in the disability community.

Creating an Inclusive Culture

How can you create a place that is welcoming and accepting of people with different abilities? Take a closer look at your hiring practices. Do you have a policy for Equal Opportunity Employment or an IDEA (Inclusion, diversity, equity, and accessibility) statement that is listed on your job postings, applications, and/or website? For your on-board process, do you encourage people to ask for accommodations? For existing employees or volunteers, is there a procedure in place for requesting accommodations as they arise? By simply adding a request form to your staff files, handbooks, or on-boarding training, you are helping to establish that culture of acceptance. All organizations, no matter how small, should have an Accessibility Coordinator, a Community Inclusion Coordinator, or a similar position. This person will be the primary contact for all things related to accessibility including staff requests, visitor accommodations, and ensuring accessible gear and trails are properly maintained. By establishing this role and assigning it to someone, you are ensuring that requests are not falling through the cracks.

Workplace Accommodations

What type of accommodations might staff or volunteers ask for? Well, that depends on their job duties. Desk items may include ergonomic chairs, standing desks, light filters or magnifiers for their screens, or for items to be emailed to them versus printing for easier reading. For outdoor positions like landscape specialists or foresters, you may be asked to limit the weight of items they are required to carry, offer adaptive gear for fishing or hunting, or provide cushions or seats for gardening to minimize bending over and squatting. Staff or volunteers may also ask for flexible schedules like reduced shift hours or the ability to work from home. This is especially helpful for people who have doctor or therapy appointments they need to attend during the day. For people who have chronic fatigue syndrome or tire easily, having the chance to work from home or adjust their schedule as needed can be beneficial. Having interpreters, communicating via email versus in-person, or including captioning on virtual meetings are ways to assist people with hearing impairments in the workplace. The best way to be inclusive and help your staff and volunteers be successful is to ask what accommodations they prefer instead of just offering something that may not be the best fit for them.

Trainings

One last recommendation is to add a training for your staff and volunteers on how to interact with people with disabilities. The trainings should include proper language to use, identifying types of physical and mental disabilities, how to interact with disabled people, and how to adapt their programs and teaching styles to assist people when needed. Offering the trainings as part of their onboarding process will ensure that everyone has received the necessary training and works to create the culture of inclusion you are striving towards.

Reflections

What are some of the key takeaways from this section?

Looking at your pre-assessment, is there something your organization currently does not offer that you think it could? Or is there something you do offer that can be improved?

Are there any barriers you need to overcome to put these practices into use? These barriers may include lack of funding, need for additional staffing, increased training for staff and volunteers, or simply not knowing where to start.

Section 5: Website Transparency

Pre-Assessment

Do you have a website?

Is it accessible (appropriate fonts, colors, clarity)?

Is it WCAG compliant?

Do you have an accessibility section on your website?

Do you have alt text for your images online?

Do you have a service dog policy? Is it stated somewhere?

Does your website list your accessible trails, facilities, and program offerings?

Is there a way to request accommodations online?

Do you have social media pages? Which ones?

Do you offer accessibility information for programs listed online or on social media?

Do you advertise with any local disability communities or groups?

Are people with disabilities represented in your advertising and marketing materials?

Website Transparency

As most marketing teams know, websites and social media accounts are an invaluable tool for most organizations. It can give a business credibility, provides a place to connect with new and returning customers, showcases your services, promotes your brand, and is a platform for all of your organization's basic information like your location, staff contacts, hours of operation, and programs. Over the past three decades since websites were first created, they have undergone many changes in styles, format, and user preferences. There are now guidelines in place for website accessibility called Website Content Accessibility Guidelines (WCAG) which assists people with vision, auditory, communication, or neurological disorders when accessing websites. The information is more technical and not covered in this guidebook but it is strongly recommended that you research it further.

Website Design Elements

When it comes to style and design, it is vital that you consider all potential users of your website, including those who may have visual impairments. If your website's background design is too busy, it may make it difficult to read. Font style, size, and color are another important factor to consider. If you have a light background, use dark font colors or if you have a dark background, use light font colors. Wording or images that are too similar in color to the background can be difficult for people with color blindness to read. Simple fonts are easier to read than elaborate or cursive fonts. Providing alt text for images allows screen readers to explain what an image is and assists people with vision impairments or cognitive disabilities access non-text information. People with certain types of epilepsy or sensory processing disorders may be sensitive to strobing lights, flickering images, popup ads, or rolling images on a screen. Minimizing special effects or having an option to turn them off is recommended.

Accessibility Section

One of the most important sections on a website for people with disabilities is often the most overlooked one: the Accessibility Section. For people who wish to visit your organization, knowing how you are accessible is just as important as knowing your business hours and address. Having information on one dedicated landing page versus scattered throughout several pages helps the visitors easily locate the information they seek. An Accessibility Section may contain information regarding accessible parking, where accessible bathrooms are located, if interpreters are available, which trails or grounds are accessible, service dog policies, where to find elevators or ramps, if adaptive gear is available for checkout, and how to request accommodations for programs or events.

Transparency

The key thing to remember is to make sure you are being transparent and honest about what your organization has and doesn't have. It is better to give a true evaluation of your buildings, trails, and programs then to end up giving someone a bad experience out of well-meaning intentions. Saying things like "mostly accessible" isn't appropriate. When in doubt, explain what you do offer. For example, you can say we have 2 miles of trails with a packed granite surface that is partly shaded with 3 benches along the path. This will allow the user to make the determination for themselves about whether that is accessible for them. When responding to requests through social media regarding accessibility, check with your Accessibility Coordinator before answering, or refer the person directly to them for further assistance.

Service Animals

Here is a quick note about service animals because some organizations or individuals seem to be confused or unaware of the laws regarding this. When in doubt, please research what the federal and state laws require. Under the Americans with Disabilities Act, service animals are dogs that are trained to assist a person with a specific disability or medical condition. Businesses open to the public are generally required to allow the service dog access to their areas, even if they don't normally allow dogs on site. Rare cases, like hospital operating rooms, are the exception to this law. The ADA requires the animal be under control of the owner at all times. Service animals are not required to have identification or wear vests, and staff cannot ask about the person's disability. You may ask if the service dog is required because of a disability and what tasks they are trained to perform. Clearly stating your service dog policy on your website is helpful for visitors and staff to avoid confusion and potential issues. There are different laws and requirements surrounding emotional support animals. When developing or modifying your organization's policy on service animals or emotional support animals, be sure research your local, state, and federal laws for the appropriate requirements.

Social Media

When creating social media posts regarding events, providing information about accessibility can be helpful. For instance, if you offer adaptive paddles for an upcoming kayaking class or if the trail your event will take place on is not wheelchair accessible, that is useful for people to know in advance. If you are offering an educational programming, let participants know how they can request accommodations for programming or who to contact with questions about accessibility. Space on social media posts, as well as the attention spans of readers, can be limited. This is where having an Accessibility Coordinator or an Accessibility Section of your website can be beneficial. Simply refer interested people to those resources for further information.

Staff Contact

Another way to demonstrate to the public and your visitors that you are inclusive is to have a way for them to contact you specifically about accessibility. On your website, marketing materials, or social media, is there a way for people to contact you regarding your accessibility or to request an accommodation for a program? As mentioned in the previous section, establishing a designated person or email address specifically dedicated to handling questions and requests regarding accessibility is invaluable for those who require it. Often when people reach out to organizations with questions, they will either get passed around between different people, receive no information, or receive incorrect information from someone who isn't sure of the answer. By designating a point of contact, all questions and requests can be funneled through that person. This way, people aren't lost in the shuffle or requests mishandled. And again, having this information clearly stated on the accessibility section of your website helps reduce the frustration of searching in multiple places just to find a simple answer.

Printed Materials

If your marketing also includes printed materials such as brochures, program guides, or tabling information for outreach, consider reviewing your products for readability. Just like with websites, the fonts, colors, and images should be chosen with usability in mind. Busy backgrounds, small wording, or cursive fonts may be difficult to read. A wonderful resource to review is the *Smithsonian Guidelines for Accessible Exhibition Design*. It is full of helpful information regarding how to create an accessible exhibit and materials and is a free download from their website.

Marketing

Lastly, consider who your marketing is geared towards. Is everyone in your pictures able-bodied people or do you feature people who are in wheelchairs, use walkers, wearing hearing aids or cochlears, using a white cane, or wearing headphones for sensory disorders? Representation in outdoor-related media is extremely important and something that is often lacking in overall diversity. Outdoor media typically features white, able-bodied, heterosexual couples enjoying nature. That sends a strong message to those who do not fall into those categories. When creating your marketing designs, think about what your images and descriptions are saying to the groups you are trying to include. Reaching out to local disability or diverse organizations for input or partnerships goes a long way in ensuring you are reaching your intended audiences in a meaningful and inclusive way.

Reflections

What are some of the key takeaways from this section?

Looking at your pre-assessment, is there something your organization currently does not offer that you think it could? Or is there something you do offer that can be improved?

Are there any barriers you need to overcome to put these practices into use? These barriers may include lack of funding, need for additional staffing, increased training for staff and volunteers, or simply not knowing where to start.

Section 6: Identifying Barriers and Organizational Goals

Barriers Faced:

As you read through each section, what were some of the barriers or limitations you identified to creating more accessible spaces and programs? Are you a government facility that must go through a long-process to approve policy changes? Are you a non-profit organization with limited funds? Do you lack the available staff needed to achieve some of your goals? Are you just not sure where to start?

Identify your barriers here:

Now, what are some ways you can overcome your barriers? Can you reach out to local volunteer groups or colleges for help or offer internships? Are there grants you can apply for related to accessibility, inclusion, diversity, or working with underserved populations? Are there any foundations who are interested in donating towards increasing accessibility in your outdoor areas? If you do have limited funds, are there items you can work on that do not require extra expenses, like adding accessibility sections to your website? Are there local organizations who would like to team up to provide volunteers or aides to help with programming?

List your ideas here:

Organizational Goals:

Look back over the pre-assessments and reflections for each section. Did you identify ways your organization can improve their accessibility in certain areas? Are there some which can be instituted immediately? Which ones require more time to establish? Using the space below, create a timeline for completing your goals. Be sure to include ways to overcome barriers, if needed. Check back every six months to track your progress. To help keep you on track, add a reminder to your calendar to check in with your timeline.

Goals Timeline:

3 months:

6 months:

1 year:

3 years:

5 years:

Track Your Progress:

Review your goals on the previous page and answer the questions below.

Which goals were you able to complete so far?

When implementing changes to policies or creating new ones, what worked well for you?

What were some of the challenges or barriers you encountered?

Did it take longer than anticipated to complete the different goals?

Did you find the resources helpful? Are there additional resources you would recommend to other organizations?

Have you received any feedback on your new practices?

RESOURCES

Americans with Disabilities Act

01

Smithsonian Guidelines for Accessible Exhibition Design

02

03

Accessibility Guidebook for Outdoor Recreation and Trails

Americans with Disabilities Act: Service Animals

04

Website Content Accessibility Guidelines (www.WCAG.com)

05

Local Lending Libraries

www.aaccessible.org/at-lending-libraries

06

Thank you!

Made in United States
Troutdale, OR
12/05/2024